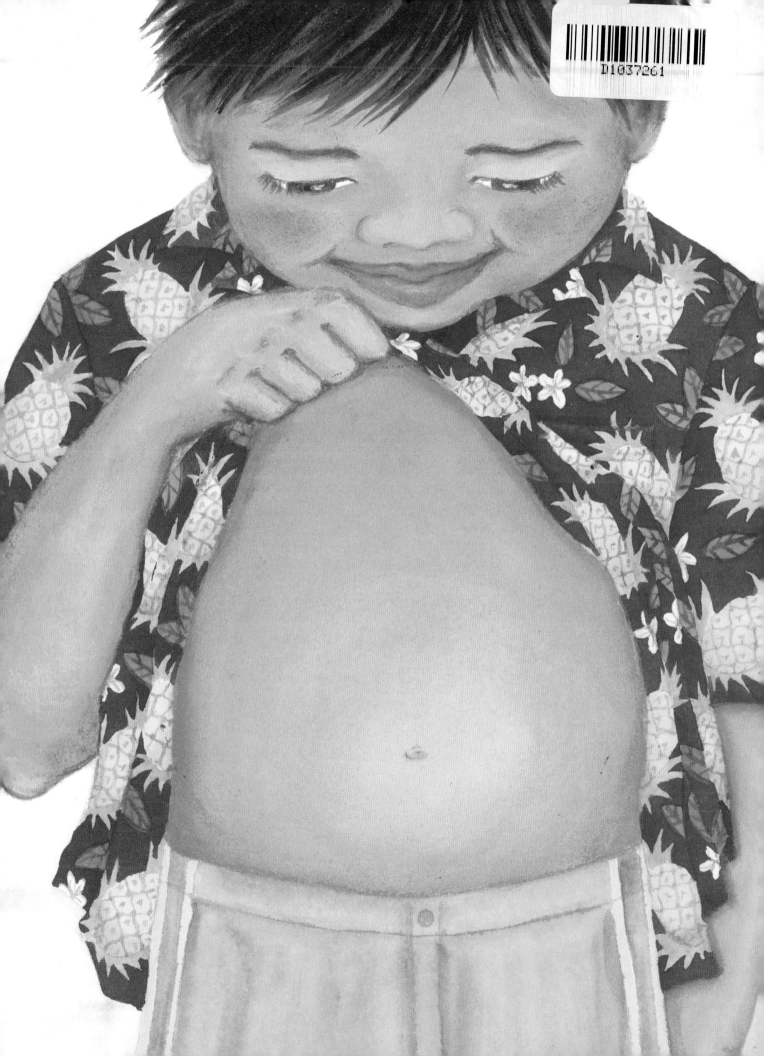
D1037261

This Is My Piko

Dedicated to
The Edith Kanaka'ole Foundation

Banana Patch Press

www.bananapatchpress.com

Text Copyright © 2009 Dr. Carolan
Illustration Copyright © 2009 Joanna F. Carolan

Library of Congress Control Number: 2007903346
ISBN: 978-0-9715333-0-1

First Edition

Printed in Hong Kong

This Is My Piko

by

Dr. Carolan

illustrated by

Joanna F. Carolan

Audio CD featuring

Nāpua Greig

Aloha keiki!
Let's learn to say
The parts of your body
You use to run and play.

As you turn each page
You will soon know,
Many Hawaiian words
From your head to your toe.

Po'o

poh-oh

Head

Po'o is your head.
You use it morning to night.
Put a hat on your po'o
When the sun is shining bright.

Lauoho

laow-oh-ho

Hair

Lauoho is your hair.
It grows out of your head.
Lauoho can be curly or straight,
Blonde, black, brown, or red.

Maka

mah-kah

Eyes

Maka are your eyes.
With them you can see
A great big rainbow
Or a small honey bee.

Ku'emaka

koo-ay-mah-kah

Eyebrows

Ku'emaka are your eyebrows.
Raise them to say hi.

Lihilihi
lee-hee-lee-hee
Eyelashes

Lihilihi are your eyelashes.
They go down when you feel shy.

Pepeiao

pay-pay-ee-ow

Ears

Pepeiao are your ears.
What is that sound?
Can you hear the ocean
In a seashell you found?

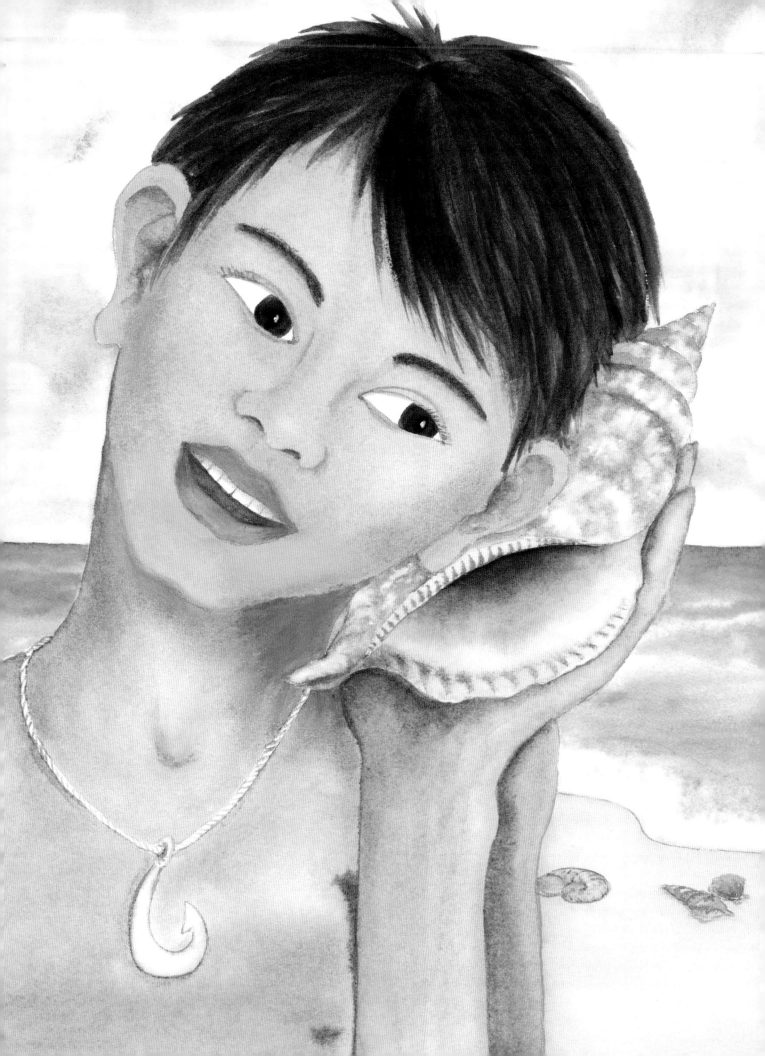

Ihu
Ee-hoo
Nose

Ihu is your nose.
And this is what I think,
Pinch your ihu closed
If you smell a bad stink!

Papālina

pah-pah-lee-nah

Cheeks

Papālina are your cheeks.
To make the balloon grow,
Puff out your papālina
And blow, blow, blow!

Waha
wah-ha
Mouth

Waha is your mouth.
Open it wide,
But only when you're singing,
Not with food inside!

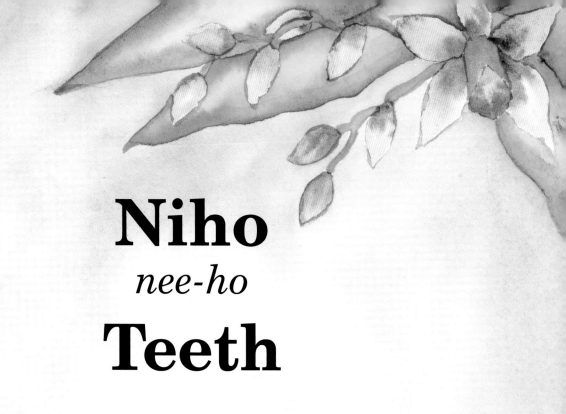

Niho

nee-ho

Teeth

Niho are your teeth.
You use them to bite.
Brush them every day
To keep your niho white.

Alelo

ah-lay-loh

Tongue

Alelo is your tongue.
Sticking it out is mean.
It's best to use your alelo
For licking an ice cream.

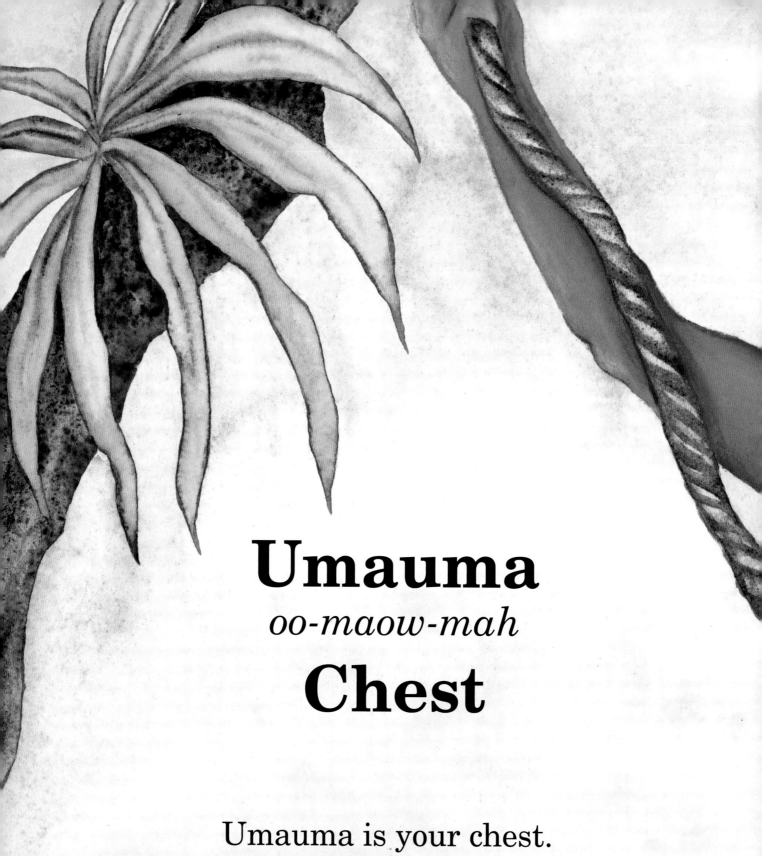

Umauma
oo-maow-mah
Chest

Umauma is your chest.
Be the jungle king.
Beat your umauma,
And ride the jungle swing!

Poʻohiwi
poh-oh-hee-vee
Shoulders

Poʻohiwi are your shoulders.
Poʻohiwi are the best
For carrying a backpack,
When baby sister needs a rest.

Ku'eku'e

koo-ay-koo-ay

Elbow

Ku'eku'e is your elbow.
Bend it back to throw.
Release it high and fast,
Or maybe low and slow.

Lima
lee-mah
Hands

Lima are your hands.
Use your lima to clap,
Or to give your friend
A high-five slap!

Manamana Lima

mah-nah-mah-nah lee-mah

Fingers

Manamana lima are your fingers.
They are very fine.
They can snap, poke, pinch and grip,
And give the shaka sign!

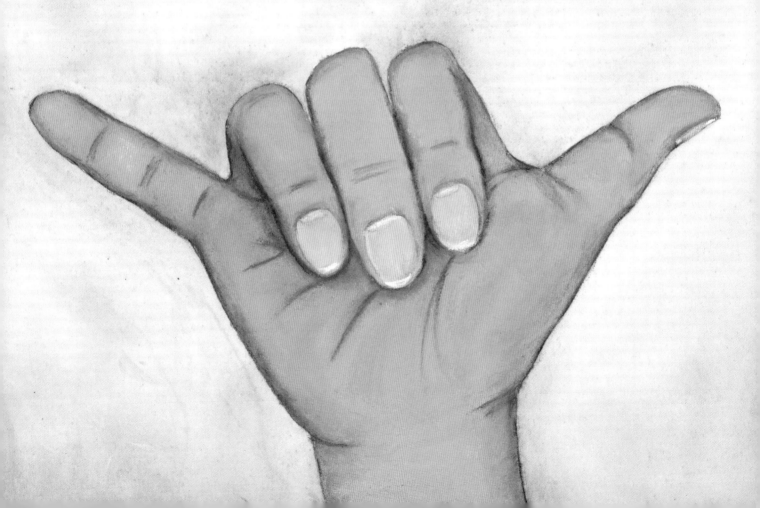

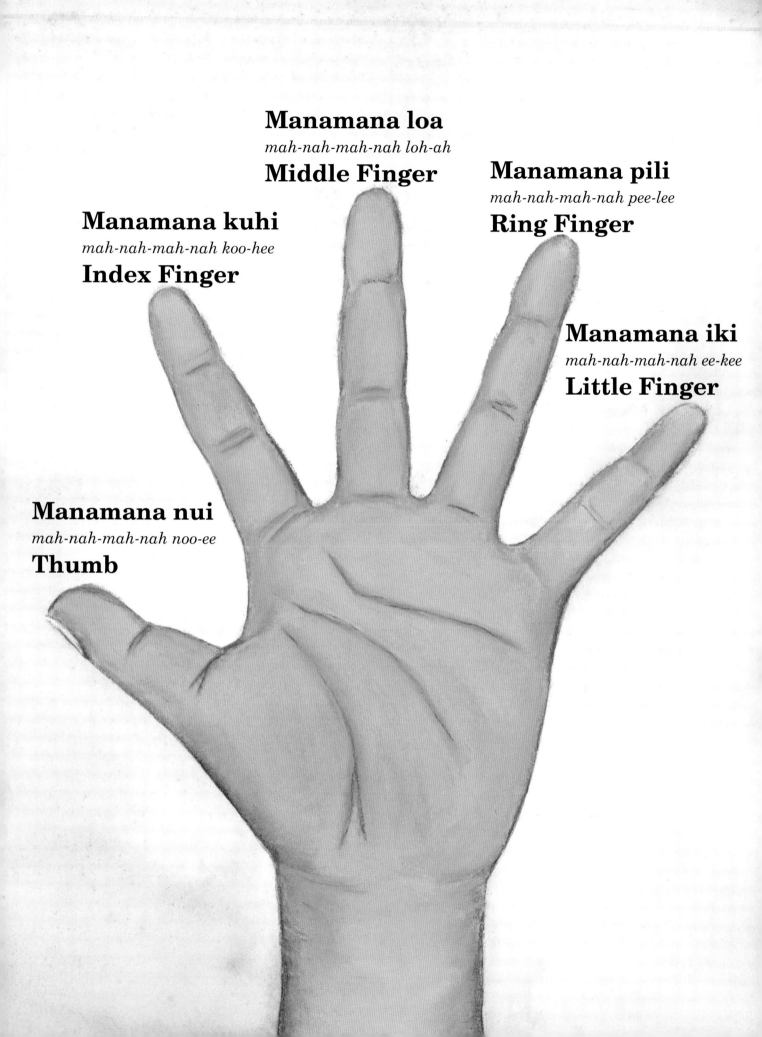

Manamana loa
mah-nah-mah-nah loh-ah
Middle Finger

Manamana pili
mah-nah-mah-nah pee-lee
Ring Finger

Manamana kuhi
mah-nah-mah-nah koo-hee
Index Finger

Manamana iki
mah-nah-mah-nah ee-kee
Little Finger

Manamana nui
mah-nah-mah-nah noo-ee
Thumb

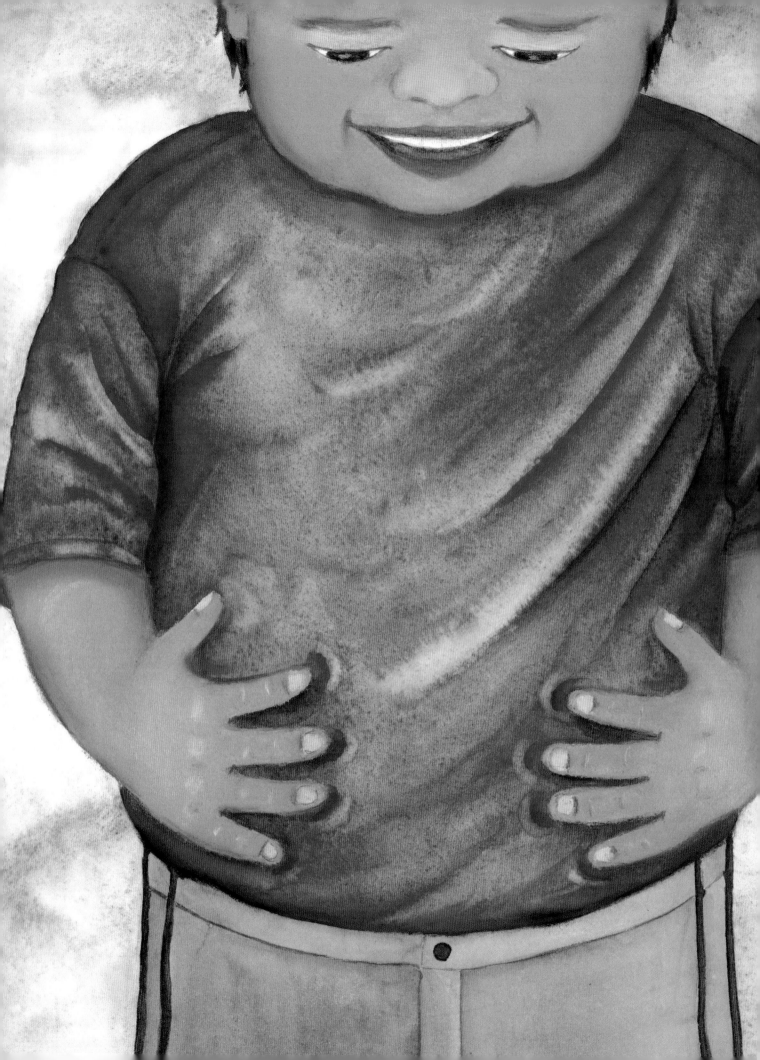

ʻŌpū

oh-poo

Belly

ʻŌpū is your belly.
When you get the giggles,
Look at your ʻōpū.
See how it jiggles!

Piko

pee-koh

Bellybutton

Piko is your bellybutton.
Can you find your piko now?
Your piko is easy to find.
Look and see how.

Kīkala
kee-kah-lah
Hips

Kīkala are your hips.
See hula dancers glide,
Swaying their kīkala,
Gracefully, side to side.

ʻĒlemu
ay-lay-moo
Bottom

'Ēlemu is your bottom.
Some are big and some are small.
See all the 'ēlemu
Sitting on the wall?

Kuli
koo-lee

Knees

Kuli are your knees.
Babies use them to crawl.
Sometimes they need a bandaid
If you take a fall.

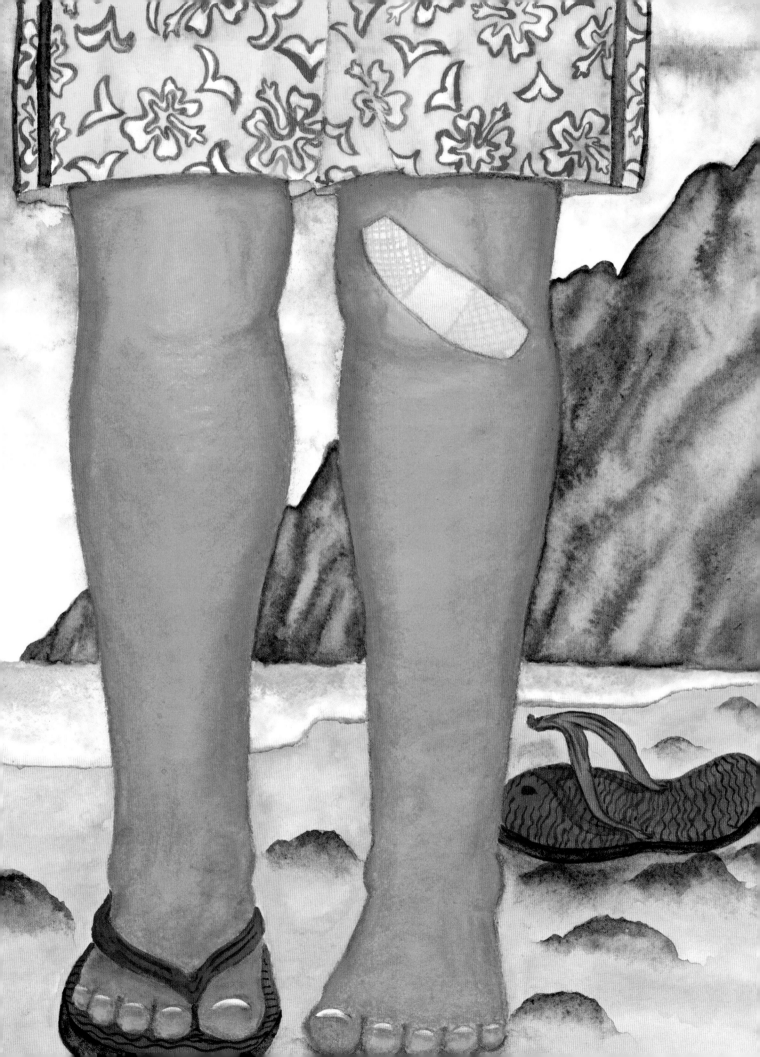

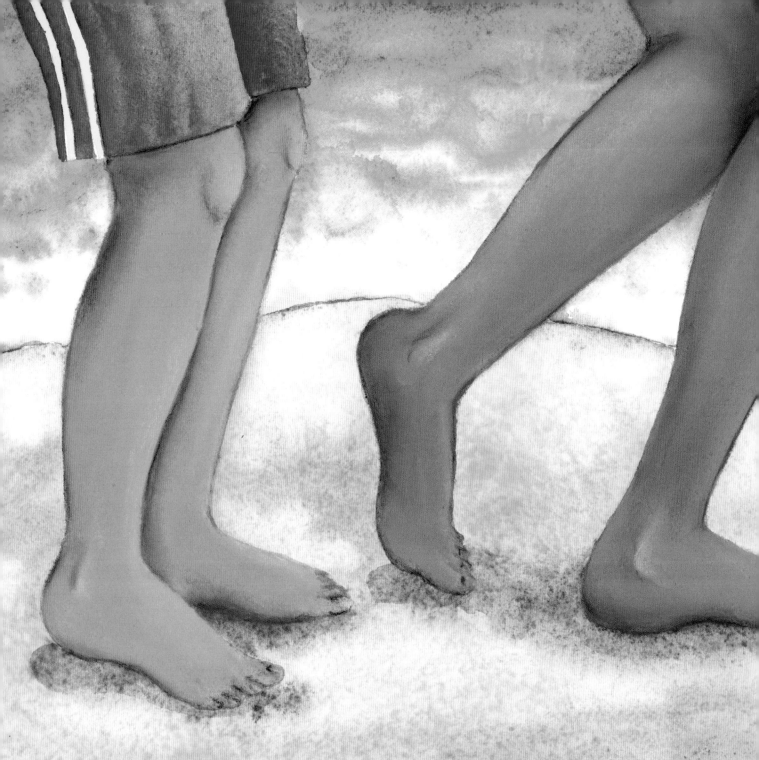

Wāwae
vah-vigh
Legs, Feet

Wāwae are your legs and feet.
You use them to walk and run.
Your wāwae do so much
Helping you have fun.

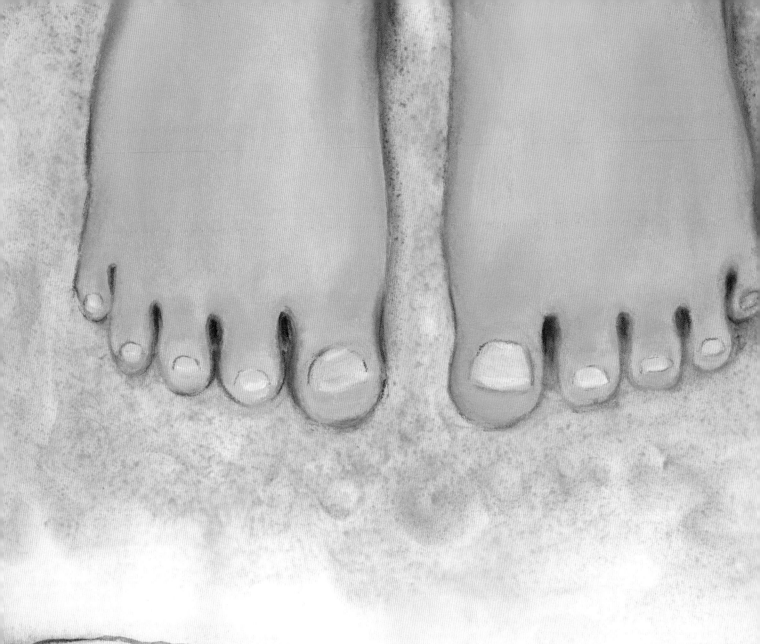

Manamana wāwae
mah-nah-mah-nah vah-vigh
Toes

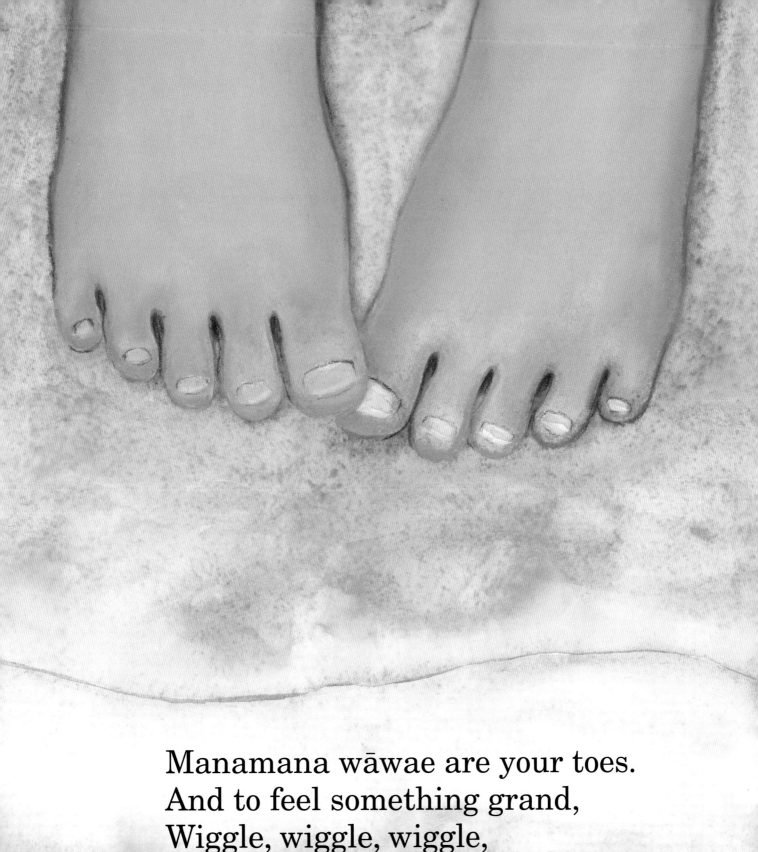

Manamana wāwae are your toes.
And to feel something grand,
Wiggle, wiggle, wiggle,
Wiggle them in the sand!

Kino

kee-noh

Body

Kino is your whole body.
Keep it healthy and strong.
And treat it with respect
Your whole life long!

EIA KOʻU KINO

This is My Body

Tell me, can you find your piko?	*bellybutton*
Just point in and there's your piko.	*bellybutton*
Yes, it's easy to find your piko	*bellybutton*
In the middle of your ʻōpū!	*belly*
Poʻo, maka, ihu, waha	*Head, eyes, nose, mouth*
Pepeiao, lima, manamana lima	*Ears, hands, fingers*
Kuli, wāwae, manamana wāwae	*Knees, feet, toes*
Me kuʻu poʻohiwi.	*With my shoulders*
Tell me, can you find your poʻo?	*head*
Just reach up and there's your poʻo.	*head*
Yes, it's easy to find your poʻo	*head*
Atop your poʻohiwi!	*shoulders*
Poʻo, maka, ihu, waha	*Head, eyes, nose, mouth*
Pepeiao, lima, manamana lima	*Ears, hands, fingers*
Kuli, wāwae, manamana wāwae	*Knees, feet, toes*
Me kuʻu poʻohiwi.	*With my shoulders*
Tell me, can you find your ihu?	*nose*
Just look down and there's your ihu.	*nose*
Yes, it's easy to find your ihu	*nose*
Right above your waha!	*mouth*
Poʻo, maka, ihu, waha	*Head, eyes, nose, mouth*
Pepeiao, lima, manamana lima	*Ears, hands, fingers*
Kuli, wāwae, manamana wāwae	*Knees, feet, toes*
Me kuʻu poʻohiwi.	*With my shoulders*

Tell me, can you find your piko?   *bellybutton*
Just point in and there's your piko.   *bellybutton*
Yes, it's easy to find your piko   *bellybutton*
In the middle of your 'ōpū!   *belly*

Poʻo, maka, ihu, waha   *Head, eyes, nose, mouth*
Pepeiao, lima, manamana lima   *Ears, hands, fingers*
Kuli, wāwae, manamana wāwae   *Knees, feet, toes*
Me kuʻu poʻohiwi.   *With my shoulders*

Tell me, can you find your lima?   *hands*
Just reach out and there's your lima.   *hands*
Now get ready to clap your lima   *hands*
Because this song is over!

Tune: *Ten Little Indian Boys*
English Verses: Dr. Carolan
Hawaiian Lyrics: Edith Kanakaʻole
Reprinted with permission from the Edith Kanakaʻole Foundation.

(L to R): Kalaʻiākea Greig, Nāpua Greig & Kaʻilihiwa Greig

About the READ ALONG CD:

Narration by: Nāpua Greig
Eia Koʻu Kino Sung by: Nāpua Greig
Eia Koʻu Kino Chorus: Nāpua Greig, Kalaʻiākea Greig & Kaʻilihiwa Greig
Slack Key Guitar & ʻUkulele: Ken Emerson
String Bass: Pancho Graham
Ipu *(gourd drum)* & ʻiliʻili *(hula percussion stones)*: Nāpua Greig

Executive Producer: Banana Patch Press
Producer: Ron Pendragon
Sound Design, Recorded, Mixed & Mastered by:
Ron Pendragon, Kauaʻi, Hawaiʻi
www.fattuesdayrecords.com

NĀPUA GREIG began dancing hula at the age of 8. Born and raised on Maui, Nāpua is a multi-talented singer, songwriter and kumu hula. In 2008 she received the prestigious Nā Hōkū Hanohano Award for "Female Vocalist of the Year". Her hula hālau, *Hālau Nā Lei Kaumaka o Uka*, has won numerous awards since she formed it in 1996, recently tying for first place in kahiko at the 2007 Merrie Monach Festival. Nāpua is also an instructor of hula, oli and Hawaiian language at Kamehameha Schools Maui. For more information visit: www.myspace.com/napuagreig

KEN EMERSON infuses style and soul into his traditional slack key and steel guitar compositions. He has been entertaining listeners around the world with his unique style for over 30 years. Recipient of the prestigious "Kahili" Award for perpetuating Hawaiian culture, Ken is also a contributing artist and composer on the first "Best Hawaiian Music Album" to win a GRAMMY® Award in 2005. For more information visit: www.kenemerson.com

PANCHO GRAHAM grew up in Kailua and played bass in the youth symphony. He lives on Kauaʻi and is a member of the esteemed musical group *Na Pali*. Graham is a composer, singer, and master of many instruments including guitar, ʻukulele and string bass. For more information visit: www.myspace.com/panchograham

DR. CAROLAN was born in Melbourne, Australia. He is a pediatrician in private practice on the island of Kaua'i, Hawai'i. He is married to Joanna F. Carolan.

JOANNA F. CAROLAN was born in San Francisco, California. She is an artist and owner of Banana Patch Studio, an art studio and gallery on Kaua'i.

Other Dr. Carolan books available from Banana Patch Press:

Ten Days in Hawaii, A Counting Book

B is for Beach, An Alphabet Book

Where Are My Slippers? A Book of Colors

Goodnight Hawaiian Moon

Old Makana Had a Taro Farm

For more information visit:
www.bananapatchpress.com
www.bananapatchstudio.com

ACKNOWLEDGMENTS

Dr. Carolan would like to thank:
My wife, Joanna Carolan
My four sons, Sean, Seumas, Brendan and Eamonn
All the keiki in my practice.

Joanna Carolan would like to thank:
My husband, Terry Carolan
The Banana Patch Studio team: Sheri, Jana, Alice, Naomi,
Michelle S., Angela, Shanelle, Brooks, Erin, Mitzi, Patty, Liselle,
Anna, Crystal, Patricia, Michelle H., Marjanne, Karl, Nancy,
Dennis, Terry, Mary, Brandee and Shar.

They would both like to thank:
Nāpua Greig
Kalaʻiākea Greig and Kaʻilihiwa Greig
Ron Pendragon
Ken Emerson
Pancho Graham
The Edith Kanakaʻole Foundation
Tom Niblick at the Printmaker, Lihue, Kauai.